The Monroe Doctrine

by Michael Burgan

Content Adviser: Mark T. Gilderhus, Ph.D.,
Lyndon Baines Johnson Chair, History Department,
Texas Christian University

Reading Adviser: Rosemary G. Palmer, Ph.D.,
Department of Literacy, College of Education,
Boise State University

Compass Point Books ✦ Minneapolis, Minnesota

Compass Point Books
3109 West 50th Street, #115
Minneapolis, MN 55410

Visit Compass Point Books on the Internet at *www.compasspointbooks.com*
or e-mail your request to *custserv@compasspointbooks.com*

On the cover: *Creating the Monroe Doctrine*, 1912 painting by Clyde Deland

Photographs ©: Bettmann/Corbis, cover, 4, 25, 38, 40; Prints Old & Rare, back cover (far left); Library of Congress, back cover, 37, 39; Three Lions/Getty Images, 5; Private Collection/Index/The Bridgeman Art Library, 6; North Wind Picture Archives, 8, 11; Austrian Archives/Corbis, 9; Collection of the New York Historical Society/The Bridgeman Art Library, 12; Collection of the Concejo Municipal, Caracas, Venezuela/Index/The Bridgeman Art Library, 14; Real Academia de Bellas Artes de San Fernando, Madrid, Spain/The Bridgeman Art Library, 15; Musée de la Ville de Paris, Musée Carnavalet, Paris, France/The Bridgeman Art Library, 16; Bildarchiv Preussischer Kulturbesitz/Art Resource, N.Y., 18; MPI/Getty Images, 19, 21; Private Collection/The Stapleton Collection/The Bridgeman Art Library, 22; *John C. Calhoun* by Charles Bird King, 1822, oil on canvas, accession number 79.1, Museum Purchase, Gallery Fund, Courtesy of Corcoran Gallery of Art, Washington, D.C./Corbis, 23; The Granger Collection, New York, 27, 32; Our Documents/National Archives and Records Administration, 28; Architect of the Capitol, 30; Portrait of Marquis de Lafayette by Matthew Harris Jouett, National Portrait Gallery, Smithsonian Institution/Art Resource, N.Y., 34; *James K. Polk* by George Peter Alexander Healy, 1846, oil on canvas, accession number 79.14, Museum Purchase, Gallery Fund, Courtesy of Corcoran Gallery of Art, Washington, D.C./Corbis, 35.

Editor: Julie Gassman
Page Production: Bobbie Nuytten
Photo Researcher: Svetlana Zhurkin
Cartographer: XNR Productions, Inc.
Library Consultant: Kathleen Baxter

Art Director: Jaime Martens
Creative Director: Keith Griffin
Editorial Director: Carol Jones
Managing Editor: Catherine Neitge

Library of Congress Cataloging-in-Publication Data
Burgan, Michael.
 The Monroe Doctrine / by Michael Burgan.
   p. cm. — (We the people)
 Includes bibliographical references and index.
 ISBN-13: 978-0-7565-2028-1 (library binding)
 ISBN-10: 0-7565-2028-2 (library binding)
 ISBN-13: 978-0-7565-2040-3 (paperback)
 ISBN-10: 0-7565-2040-1 (paperback)
1. Monroe doctrine—Juvenile literature. 2. United States—Foreign relations—1817-1825—Juvenile literature. I. Title. II. Series.
 JZ1482.B87 2006
 327.7308—dc22   2006027089

TABLE OF CONTENTS

A Message for Europe

Less than 50 years after declaring its independence, the young United States had a message for the world: Stay away. Do not plan on establishing any more colonies in North and South America. Do not interfere in our "New World." This unexpected strong stand pushed the United States toward becoming a major player in world affairs.

James Monroe served as U.S. president from 1817 to 1825.

The bold statement to the world was made on December 2, 1823, when the U.S. Congress met to hear the annual message of President James Monroe. For part of his message, Monroe—who

4

was the fifth president of the United States—discussed American relations with foreign countries. The president and his advisers were mainly worried about two countries, Russia and France. Russia controlled Alaska and wanted to extend its lands farther south. France, some Americans feared, was preparing to invade Spain. If it did, the French might try to end the revolutions taking place in Spain's

The main street of Russian America's capital, Sitka, featured a Russian-Greek church. Russian America was the name given to Russia's territory in Alaska.

5

South American colonies—revolutions that Monroe and most Americans supported.

In his message, Monroe told Congress—and the world—that the United States would not accept new European colonies in North America. The president saw

José de San Martin (on white horse), a leader of the revolutions in South America, is a national hero in Argentina.

6

the New World of North and South America as distinct from the "Old World" of Europe. The United States, Monroe said, would not interfere with events that took place in Europe. In return, he expected the European nations to stay out of the affairs of New World nations. The president's statement on foreign policy was later called the Monroe Doctrine.

The United States did not have the military power to prevent European military forces from taking action in North or South America. Still, the Monroe Doctrine showed that the United States was taking an active role in world affairs. And it let Europe know that Americans saw the Western Hemisphere as their concern, not Europe's. Later presidents would add new ideas to the doctrine that strengthened the U.S. claim to be the major power in the region.

SEARCHING FOR PEACE

Nine years before Monroe's famous speech, Europeans and Americans were at peace. In Belgium, British and American diplomats worked on a treaty to end the War of 1812—a two-and-a-half-year war fought in North America and at sea.

Meanwhile, a series of European wars, which had begun in the late 18th century, also came to a temporary end in 1814. Great Britain and its European allies defeated the French army led by Napoléon Bonaparte. European diplomats met in

A handbill announced the signing of the Treaty of Ghent, which ended the War of 1812.

Vienna, Austria, to discuss the future of their continent. They wanted to ensure that kings once again ruled in lands that France had conquered over the course

A 19th-century illustration featured the Congress of Vienna, where European leaders formed the Holy Alliance.

of the European wars.

In Vienna, Alexander I of Russia called for a Holy Alliance to unite the most powerful Christian nations of Europe. Austria and Prussia joined the Holy Alliance, and a second alliance with Great Britain was created to maintain peace in Europe. Except for another brief war with France in 1815, this Quadruple Alliance of Great Britain, Austria, Prussia, and Russia did keep the peace—for a time.

9

THE SITUATION IN SOUTH AMERICA

One of the countries France conquered during the European wars was Spain. That victory gave Spanish colonists in South America the chance to create their own governments. With France's support, the colonists took control from local Spanish officials. Many South Americans wanted republican governments—the same kind of government the United States had. Most European rulers, however, favored kingdoms. They knew that giving people the right to choose their leaders would destroy the power of monarchies.

In addition to spreading republican ideas, the changes in South America helped American businesses. Under Spanish rule, South Americans could not trade freely with the rest of the world. Their natural resources went to Spain, and they had to buy goods from Spanish merchants. The new independence meant the South Americans could

Items like coffee beans made Brazil a favorable trading partner for North Americans.

trade with U.S. merchants. The Americans who made
money with this trade wanted to recognize the new South
American nations. If the United States officially recognized
the new governments, the existence and independence of
each of the countries would be acknowledged and accepted.

President James Monroe, however, ignored the call
to recognize any governments in South America. He had
another concern. In 1819, his chief adviser on foreign

John Quincy Adams

relations, Secretary of State John Quincy Adams, was holding talks with Spanish diplomats. The United States already owned most of Florida, and Adams was trying to gain the rest of it from Spain. The secretary also wanted to set the boundary between the United States and Mexico, which Spain owned as well. If Monroe had recognized the independent South American governments, Spain may have grown upset and Adams' work would have been ruined.

However, by the end of 1821, Adams' deals with Spain were done, and President Monroe was willing to recognize Colombia and Chile. In the spring of 1822, Argentina and Mexico were also recognized. These four

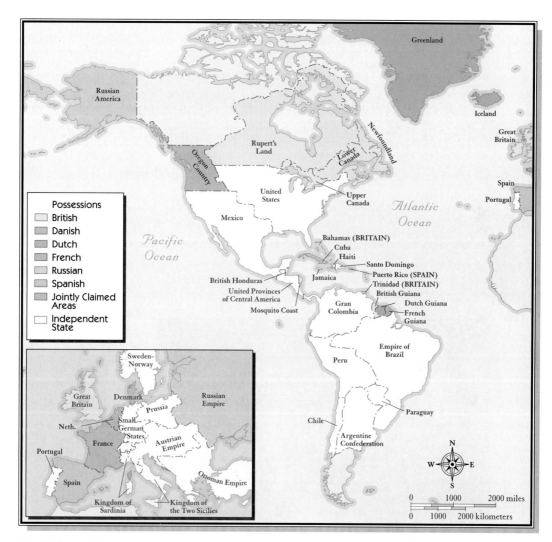

By 1823, much of South America was divided into independent nations.

new nations had been carved out of Spain's colonial lands.
Spain protested Monroe's action, but soon the United States
was receiving diplomats from these nations.

13

BACK IN EUROPE

When France had conquered Spain, Ferdinand VII was removed as Spain's king. But when France was defeated in 1814, the major European nations put Ferdinand VII back on Spain's throne. Once back in power, Ferdinand wanted to regain control over the South American colonies and destroy the republican governments there.

In 1811, Argentina became one of the first South American countries to sign a Declaration of Independence from Spain.

In 1820, the king prepared to send troops to South America. His soldiers, however, had been facing horrible living conditions, and they rebelled against his leadership. Soon citizens in Spain who opposed Ferdinand joined this rebellion. To restore order, Ferdinand had to accept a new constitution. The document weakened the king's power and gave more power to the people.

Ferdinand VII of Spain

The rebellion in Spain startled the members of the Holy Alliance. Republican revolts were already breaking out in Portugal, Italy, and Greece. The leaders of Europe wanted to protect the rule of kings, and they were ready to use military might to do so. In 1821, Austrian troops ended the revolts in Italy, and in October 1822, the Holy Alliance decided to send French

15

troops into Spain. France was now ruled by a king who was allied with Austria, Prussia, and Russia. The French troops would support Ferdinand and end the republican government he had been forced to accept.

In April 1823, French troops marched into Spain.

In August 1823, the French handed the Spanish rebels a defeat at the Battle of Trocadero. Less than one month later, France had restored power to Ferdinand.

Some Americans began to fear that the French would not stop with just restoring King Ferdinand's power. The French might also sail across the Atlantic and try to destroy the new South American countries. Although the British were not eager to have new republican governments in South America, they shared the Americans' concern. Like the United States, Great Britain made money trading with the new nations and did not want France sending troops to squash the independence of the former Spanish colonies.

In August, a British diplomat suggested to an American diplomat that the Americans and British work together to stop the French from invading South America. He proposed that the two countries publicly declare their plan to work against the French.

Meanwhile, the United States had another foreign relations problem. Russia had been expanding farther south from Alaska. The Russians had begun to live there in the late 18th century. In 1812, Russian settlers had built a fort in what is now northern California. At the same time, Americans were trading with Indians in lands Russia claimed.

In September 1821, Russian leader Alexander I tried to end the U.S. trading. He said that foreign ships could not come within 100 miles (160 kilometers) of Russia's territory in North America. He also said that Russia's territory reached as far south as the 51st line of latitude. The supposed border was well into the Oregon Country, land that both Great Britain and the United States claimed.

In July 1823, Secretary Adams met with Baron Tuyl, the Russian diplomacy minister to the United States. Adams expressed his anger

Alexander I

18

Russia's fort in California, known as Fort Ross, served as a fur trading post.

with the new Russian policy. He said, "The American
continents are no longer subjects for any new European
colonial establishments." The United States recognized the
right of Great Britain to have its colony of Canada. But
the rest of North and South America, Adams said, should
be under local control. Tuyl hoped Russia and the United
States could use diplomacy to settle the issue.

RESPONDING TO THE BRITISH

Diplomacy was a slow process in the 1820s. Without telephones or the Internet, diplomats had to send letters to their home countries. Messages from Europe could take weeks to cross the Atlantic Ocean by ship. So it wasn't until October 1823 that President Monroe learned about the proposal for the United States and Great Britain to jointly declare their intention to stop the French from going into South America. But before making a decision on this, Monroe asked Thomas Jefferson and James Madison for their opinions.

Madison and Jefferson were two of Monroe's closest friends in politics. Both men were former presidents with great knowledge of foreign affairs. Jefferson told Monroe that the United States should work with the British. A joint declaration, he believed, would be enough to stop France from risking a war in South America.

Madison shared Jefferson's views. "With [British]

Monroe sent Jefferson a letter to ask his advice about the proposed partnership with Great Britain.

cooperation," he wrote, "we have nothing to fear from the rest of Europe, and with it the best assurance of success." But Madison did not think the message should stop there.

He also wanted Monroe to speak out against the French military action in Spain and to tell the European powers to stay out of Greece, where rebels were battling for independence from the huge Ottoman Empire. Many Americans at the time supported the Greek rebels, who hoped to form a republican government.

Greece's battle for independence began in 1821 and lasted until 1829.

Along with the advice of his two friends, Monroe turned to his Cabinet for ideas on what to do. On November 7, the president met with Secretary of State Adams, Secretary of the Navy Samuel Southard, and Secretary of War John C. Calhoun. For two and a half hours, the four debated the British proposal.

John C. Calhoun

Calhoun was the strongest supporter of making a declaration with Great Britain against the Holy Alliance. In contrast, Adams wanted a strong stance against the alliance without making a joint statement with the British. Adams may have been thinking about his future political career. He was already planning to run for president in 1824. One historian has argued that Adams did not want to be associated with any foreign policy that might upset large numbers of voters. Many Americans were still angry with Great Britain because of the War of 1812 and did not want to work with them.

At the meeting, the men did not reach any decisions. Afterward, Adams remained behind for more discussions with Monroe. Adams believed that the president had to explain the U.S. position on all the important issues it faced. Monroe agreed, but he would need several more weeks to decide exactly what he should say.

During that time, his fears about French activity in South America grew. France had taken control of Spain. Rumors spread that French ships were already preparing to sail to South America. Adams, however, did not think the Holy Alliance would take action against the former Spanish colonies. He said it was as likely that Chimborazo, a huge South American mountain, "will sink beneath the ocean."

A NEW DOCTRINE

On November 21, Monroe met again with his Cabinet. The president had decided that the United States should make its own statement protesting any European involvement in South America. He rejected the idea of a joint declaration

Monroe stood among his Cabinet members in a 1912 painting of the creation of the Monroe Doctrine.

25

with Great Britain. The president also wished to address other points in the statement. He wanted to criticize France for its invasion of Spain, express support for Greek independence, and voice opposition to European colonies in North America—the policy Adams had first introduced to Baron Tuyl of Russia.

On November 22, Adams met privately with Monroe. He thought some of the language in the president's proposed statement was too strong. He feared Monroe's views could lead to war with the Holy Alliance. Adams said Monroe's main point should be "against the interference of the European powers by force with South America, but to disclaim all interference on our part with Europe." He believed that countries in each hemisphere should not interfere with the affairs of the other.

After making changes to his annual address, Monroe had it delivered to Congress. He was not present on December 2 when his written message was read to the lawmakers.

The U.S. House, as painted in 1822 by artist and famed inventor Samuel F.B. Morse

The doctrine first addressed the concerns over Russian expansion in North America. Monroe told Congress that both the United States and Great Britain hoped to keep friendly relations with Russia and settle their differences. But he also said that "the American continents … are henceforth not to be considered as subjects for future colonization by any European powers." With that statement, Monroe echoed what Adams had told Baron Tuyl several months

the condition of the people of those countries; and that it appeared to be conducted with extraordinary moderation. It need scarcely be remarked, that the result has been, so far, very different from what was then anticipated. Of events in that quarter of the Globe, with which we have so much intercourse, and from which we derive our origin, we have always been anxious and interested spectators. The Citizens of the United States cherish sentiments the most friendly, in favor of the liberty and happiness of their fellow men on that side of the Atlantic. In the wars of the European powers, in matters relating to themselves, we have never taken any part, nor does it comport with our policy so to do. It is only when our rights are invaded, or seriously menaced, that we resent injuries, or make preparation for our defence. With the movements in this Hemisphere we are of necessity more immediately connected, and by causes which must be obvious to all enlightened and impartial observers. The political system of the allied

A page of James Monroe's original handwritten annual address

before. Now, however, the idea of no new European colonies in the Americas became official U.S. policy.

Monroe also noted that violence had broken out in Europe as citizens tried to form new governments. Americans, he said, welcomed "the liberty and happiness of their fellowmen on that side of the Atlantic." But the United States would not get involved in European wars. "It is only when our rights are invaded or seriously menaced," Monroe explained, "that we make preparation for our defense."

The president then outlined the differences between Europe and the Americas. The United States and the former Spanish colonies had republican governments, while the Europeans had kingdoms. Americans cherished the government they had fought so hard to build. Monroe said the United States would consider any efforts by Europeans to bring kingdoms to the Americas "as dangerous to our peace and safety." But he assured the Europeans that the United States would not try to interfere with existing European colonies in the New World, such as the British colony in Canada.

29

THE MONROE DOCTRINE · 1823

The Monroe Doctrine is one theme in a series of ceiling paintings in the U.S. Capitol. The works were painted in the 1970s by artist Allyn Cox.

In his message, Monroe had taken some of Adams' advice. He did not specifically address France's invasion of Spain, and he weakened his show of support for the Greek rebels. In addition, he accepted Adams' strong position against a joint declaration with Great Britain, rejecting Jefferson and Madison's advice to the contrary.

30

Some historians have said that Adams was the true author of the Monroe Doctrine. Yet Monroe used the advice of many people. And he rejected Adams' wish to keep the message private. Monroe chose to make these important statements in public.

The president hoped his message would show the world that the United States was an independent power. Though Monroe did not rule out working with the British in the future, he wanted to make a strong statement. Acting on its own, he told Jefferson, "would place [the United States] on more independent and honorable ground."

REACTION TO THE DOCTRINE

The president's warning to Europe to stay out of the
Americas filled many Americans with pride. Some ignored
the fact, however, that the United States lacked the military

*An early 20th-century political cartoon points out that the Monroe Doctrine told
European leaders to keep their "hands off" the Western Hemisphere.*

strength to support Monroe's bold words. Also, no one knew that Great Britain and France had already come to an agreement. Not wanting to risk war with the British and its powerful navy, France agreed not to invade South America. News of the agreement spread around Europe at about the same time Monroe's words did.

Some British newspapers welcomed the Monroe Doctrine. They thought it showed that Great Britain and the United States had similar views on the Holy Alliance. Others saw the doctrine as Monroe's attempt to keep the British out of the Oregon Country.

In the Holy Alliance nations, the leaders spoke harshly against the new doctrine. But the doctrine found a friend in France. The Marquis de Lafayette had helped Americans fight for independence against Great Britain. He also supported republican governments in general. He called the doctrine, "The best little bit of paper that God ever permitted any man to give to the World."

Americans thought South Americans would welcome

France's Marquis de Lafayette supported the doctrine.

the Monroe Doctrine. Many South American leaders, however, realized that it was British naval power that had saved them from French attack. And some of the leaders did not think Monroe had their best interests in mind. They believed the Americans wanted to keep Europeans out of South America so the United States could control affairs there.

THE DOCTRINE AFTER MONROE

The end of the French threat meant Monroe did not have to act on his new doctrine. He left the presidency in 1825, and no president after him was required to carry out his policies. But during the 1840s, President James Polk looked back to Monroe's statement. The United States hoped to acquire Texas, all of the Oregon Country, and California. Polk feared that European nations might try to stop them. He cited the Monroe Doctrine while warning Europeans not to establish new colonies in North America.

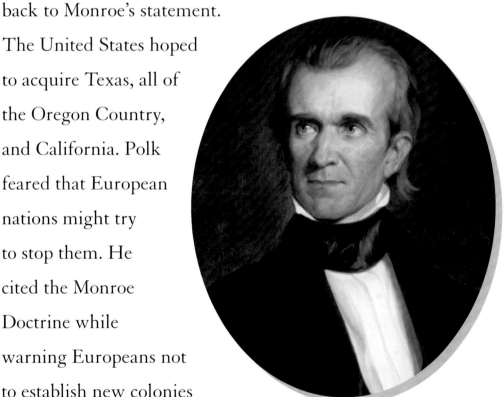

President James Polk served from 1845 to 1849.

35

Then during the 1860s, some Americans pointed to the Monroe Doctrine when they wanted to invade Mexico. France had replaced the government there with a king it had chosen—an action that directly conflicted with the policy of the Monroe Doctrine. After the U.S. Civil War, American troops prepared to fight the French, but the Mexicans drove them out on their own.

In 1895, troubles in Venezuela led President Grover Cleveland to refer to the Monroe Doctrine. Venezuela bordered the British colony of Guiana, but there was a disagreement over the boundary between the two. The United States backed Venezuela and demanded that Great Britain settle the South American dispute. Some Americans were ready to go to war if Great Britain refused, but the British accepted Cleveland's demands.

Six years later, President Theodore Roosevelt called the Monroe Doctrine "a guarantee of the commercial independence of the Americas." He saw that economic troubles in a South or Central American nation might

*An 1896 cartoon showed an armed Uncle Sam standing between
European leaders and citizens of Venezuela.*

lead to European involvement. In 1903, Germany attacked

Venezuela when it refused to pay its debts. Roosevelt

convinced the Germans to settle the problem peacefully.

Rather than have such future situations, Roosevelt

created a new role for the United States. It would be the

policeman of the Western Hemisphere. Before troubles

within a country led to violence, the United States would

37

President Roosevelt was prepared to protect South and Central American countries if needed.

step in. Roosevelt had created what was called a corollary, or natural addition, to the Monroe Doctrine.

After the Roosevelt Corollary, many U.S. presidents

argued that they could send troops into Central or South America to preserve peace. Often, the troops also defended the interests of U.S. businesses in those countries. Within the next decade, the United States became one of the most powerful countries in the world.

President Woodrow Wilson could not accept one part of the Monroe Doctrine—staying out of European affairs. He helped the British during World War I, which the United States entered in 1917. Wilson said he wanted to expand a main idea of the Monroe Doctrine to include the entire world. "No nation," he said, "should seek to extend its polity

President Woodrow Wilson served from 1913 to 1921.

39

[government] over any other nation or people."

After World War II ended in 1945, the United States had one major enemy: the Soviet Union. For decades, the two countries sought to spread their influence around the world. At times, U.S. presidents cited the Monroe Doctrine as they tried to keep the Soviets out of the Western Hemisphere.

In 1962, the Soviet Union placed missiles in Cuba,

President John F. Kennedy met with his advisers to discuss the missiles in Cuba.

only 90 miles (144 km) from Florida. These missiles were powerful enough to destroy entire American cities. U.S. leaders discussed the Monroe Doctrine as President John F. Kennedy debated what to do about the missiles. Rather than attack Cuba, Kennedy used diplomacy to make the Soviets remove the missiles and end the crisis.

In 1991, the Soviet Union collapsed. Some historians say the Monroe Doctrine ended that year, too. No country in the world had the military power to threaten U.S. interests in the Western Hemisphere. But during its long history, the doctrine helped shape the United States and other countries in the Americas.

GLOSSARY

Cabinet—a president's group of advisers who are the heads of government departments

commercial—relating to business

Congress—the branch of the United States government that makes laws, consisting of the House of Representatives and the Senate

constitution—a document stating the basic rules of a government

diplomats—people who manage a country's affairs with other nations

latitude—distance measured north or south of the equator; each degree of latitude equals about 69 miles (110 km)

Ottoman Empire—a former nation that included parts of Africa, Asia, and Europe, centered on modern-day Turkey

republican—governed by leaders elected by the people to represent them

secretary—a person who leads a government department

Western Hemisphere—the half of the globe that contains North and South America and the surrounding waters

42

DID YOU KNOW?

- From 1811 to 1817, James Monroe served as secretary of state for President James Madison.

- After serving as secretary of state for Monroe, John Quincy Adams was elected president in 1824. Adams' father had been president from 1797 to 1801.

- George Washington gave the first yearly presidential message to Congress in person. Jefferson was the first president to have it read. The tradition of the president delivering the address in person started again with Woodrow Wilson in 1913.

- The Monroe Doctrine is not part of international law. The United States had no legal right to demand that European nations stay out of the Western Hemisphere.

- In 1948, the United States joined 20 other nations in the Western Hemisphere to form the Organization of American States. Its goals include defending the region from outside attack and ending disagreements among members.

IMPORTANT DATES

Timeline

1814 Great Britain and the United States end the War of 1812.

1815 Major European nations create the Holy Alliance and the Quadruple Alliance.

1819 Spain agrees to turn Florida over to the United States to end a border dispute.

1821 Alexander I of Russia extends his country's claims to land in North America; President James Monroe recognizes the independence of two new nations formed in former Spanish lands.

1822 The Holy Alliance decides to send French troops into Spain to help the king there.

1823 In August, Great Britain proposes a joint declaration with the United States warning France not to invade South America; in December, President Monroe presents the Monroe Doctrine, telling European nations to stay out of the Western Hemisphere.

1904 President Theodore Roosevelt offers a corollary to the Monroe Doctrine, claiming the United States has the right to keep peace within Central and South America.

IMPORTANT PEOPLE

JOHN QUINCY ADAMS (1767–1848)

Secretary of state who influenced the writing of the Monroe Doctrine and later became the sixth U.S. president; his nickname was "Old Man Eloquent," in reference to his superb speaking skills

ALEXANDER I (1777–1825)

Ruler of Russia from 1801 to 1825 and founder of the Holy Alliance

FERDINAND VII (1784–1833)

King of Spain from 1808 to 1833; during his reign the Spanish colonies in the New World were lost

JAMES MONROE (1758–1831)

Fifth president of the United States; before serving as president, he fought in the Revolutionary War and served as a senator, diplomat, secretary of state, and secretary of war

JAMES POLK (1795–1849)

Eleventh president of the United States and the first to refer to the Monroe Doctrine; Texas was added to the United States during his presidency

THEODORE ROOSEVELT (1858–1919)

Twenty-sixth president of the United States and author of the Roosevelt Corollary, an addition to the Monroe Doctrine

WANT TO KNOW MORE?

At the Library

Burgan, Michael. *John Quincy Adams.* Minneapolis: Compass Point Books, 2003.

Greenblatt, Miriam. *Napoleon Bonaparte and Imperial France.* New York: Marshall Cavendish Benchmark Books, 2005.

Richie, Jason. *Secretaries of State: Making Foreign Policy.* Minneapolis: Oliver Press, 2002.

Santella, Andrew. *James Monroe: America's 5th President.* New York: Children's Press, 2003.

On the Web

For more information on this topic, use FactHound.

1. Go to *www.facthound.com*

2. Type in this book ID: 0756520282

3. Click on the *Fetch It* button.

FactHound will find the best Web sites for you.

On the Road

Ash Lawn-Highland

1000 James Monroe Parkway

Charlottesville, VA 22902-8722

434/293-9539

The home of James Monroe

U.S. Capitol

Washington, DC 20515

202/225-6827

The building where Congress works and where the Monroe Doctrine was first read

Look for more We the People books about this era:

The Alamo

The Arapaho and Their History

The Battle of the Little Bighorn

The Buffalo Soldiers

The California Gold Rush

California Ranchos

The Cherokee and Their History

The Chumash and Their History

The Creek and Their History

The Erie Canal

Great Women of Pioneer America

Great Women of the Old West

The Iroquois and Their History

The Klondike Gold Rush

The Lewis and Clark Expedition

The Library of Congress

The Louisiana Purchase

The Mexican War

The Ojibwe and Their History

The Oregon Trail

The Pony Express

The Powhatan and Their History

The Pueblo and Their History

The Santa Fe Trail

The Sioux and Their History

The Trail of Tears

The Transcontinental Railroad

The Wampanoag and Their History

The War of 1812

The Wilderness Road

A complete list of We the People titles is available on our Web site:
www.compasspointbooks.com

INDEX

About the Author

Michael Burgan is a freelance writer for children and adults. A history graduate of the University of Connecticut, he has written more than 100 fiction and nonfiction children's books for various publishers. For adult audiences, he has written news articles, essays, and plays. Michael Burgan is a recipient of an Educational Press Association of America award.